Taking the innocence

from the sunshine

by

Lytoni S. Brown

wwww.unspokenwordspublishing.com

Copyright © 2010 Lytoni S. Brown

All rights reserved. No part of this book may be reproduced in any form without written permission from the publisher.

ISBN: 978-0-9771358-3-7

Published by:
Unspoken Words Publishing

wwww.unspokenwordspublishing.com

Other books by Lytoni S. Brown:
Transformation

Dear reader,

Thank you for supporting my book. I have been writing this book for five years, and it holds some of my deepest thoughts. It was so hard to release my words, and it was easier to keep my unspoken words inside of me. Jesus Christ, Unspoken Words Publishing, the two books I wrote, and telling someone about my story was my pathway to freedom. Even afterwards, I still battle a lot of emotions, and it's still hard for me to obtain good relationships. I just learn how to take it day-by-day and trust in God that He will bring me out 'cause my life can't end in my molestation. I have read books, watched movies, and heard stories of adult survivors of molestation but never knew where to go. It was so hard for me to find my way out. I started Unspoken Words Publishing, so my voice could be heard. I wanted Unspoken Words Publishing to be the now-what-do-I-do-from here center. Unspoken Words will provide the tools that I know work, such as online group discussions, books, local support groups, and names of professional counselors. Remembering what the letters TEAM mean together—everyone achieves more, so please work with me and post your comments or concerns at

http://wwww.unspokenwordspublishing.com.

Beautiful Flower

SUNSHINE WAS SEVEN YEARS OLD; she was the eldest out of three kids. Sunshine was shiny; she had brown skin, brown eyes, long black hair, full lips, long fingers, and big feet. Sunshine was the mother of the house. She took care of her sisters while her mother was at work and out partying. She cooked; she cleaned; she got both of her sisters dressed for school, walked them to school, and picked them up from school. She tried her best to be her mother to her sisters.

Sunshine's mother was shiny. She had brown skin, brown eyes, long black hair, full lips, long fingers, and big feet. Sunshine looked like her twin. And her twin she wanted to be. Her mother worked from nine to six, came home, and slept for two hours. She woke up around 8:00 to get ready to go to the club; around 10:00, she was off to the club. At that time, Sunshine would bathe all her sisters, put them all to sleep, and wait for her mother to get home from her dissension. Sunshine would always stay awake; if she was to drift off to sleep, she would wake up intensely. She would run to her mother's door. Nine times out of ten, the door would be closed; and she would hear moans, groans, and "oh, baby." At that point, she knew her mother made it home safely. She would go into her bedroom and masturbate off the noise that came from the other room.

One Saturday morning after her mother came home from a party, Sunshine saw a man come out of her mother's room, which was unusual because all of her mother's men would leave the house around 5:00 or 6:00 in the morning before she and her other siblings would wake up for school. Her mother came out of the room, half-naked, and said, "Kids, this is Henry; and Henry, this is Lashay, Tasha, and my eldest daughter Sunshine. Henry said hi to all of them, and her mother went to bed while Henry stayed in the living room and talked to all of the girls. Sunshine was happy to see a man her mother dated. She had never seen a man her mother had dated—not even her own father.

Henry stayed around for a while. He would buy the girls things, give them money to go to the store, and even buy them candy. Once her mother met Henry, she stopped going out as much and spent more time at home, pretending to be a family. Henry studied each girl like a book: Lashay, the youngest, had a big mouth. She tried to boss her two older sisters like she was the oldest. Tasha was a fighter; she was ready to fight over every little thing. Sunshine still acted like the mother of the house because that was what she was used to doing for so long. Her mother tried to stop her and told her to act like a child. But she did not know how to be a child because she was an adult for the last five years of her

Taking the Innocence from the Sunshine 9

life. Sunshine's mother had all the girls call Henry "daddy" to make her picture perfect family complete.

One day, Sunshine's mother went to the doctor and left Henry to watch the girls. Henry was in the basement, getting high off the white rock; Lashay and Tasha were outside playing while Sunshine was watching a movie. Henry came up stairs, sat next to Sunshine high as a kite, and asked her, "How much do you love your mother?"

Sunshine replied, "Words cannot explain how much I love her. When I grow up, I am going to be just like her."

Henry moved closer to Sunshine and said, "Do you want to be just like her?"

Sunshine said, "Yes."

Henry took a sip of his beer and started to kiss Sunshine on the lips. She tasted the beer from his tongue. He said, "Do you want to be just like your mother?" as he felt her young body up and down.

She said, "Yes," as she moaned and groaned like she heard her mother do behind closed doors.

He kissed her neck down to her doorknobs and placed her innocents into his mouth. He pulled his manhood out and told her to kiss it like she had never kissed before. After she French kissed his manhood, he penetrated her, breaking her innocents to pieces. It was so painful to her; and he said, "I am making you into your mother. You want to be her, right?"

Sunshine replied, "Yes, Daddy," with painful tears in her eyes, but then she pictured her mother's face and that helped her endure the pain.

He pulled out and spilled his kids all over her. He told her get and wash up while he cleaned up the mess she made. Sunshine got into the shower, knowing she had just become her mother.

When she got out of the shower, her mother was on the couch where Sunshine had become her and said, "Baby, I am pregnant."

Five years later, Henry woke up early one Sunday morning and took the family to church. The girls went to children's church, and Henry and Tonya went to regular church. After hearing the Word of God delivered, it moved Henry into salvation. The man of God preached that God can save the worst sinner. Henry tried to stay away from church because of his lifestyle; but when he heard God can save a sinner, he knew that was his way out of the chains and jail cells over his life. Henry felt like a dead man alive, looking for restoration through any source.

He went from women, to alcohol, to drugs, to a little girl; and his soul was still lost. He could not find peace in any

Taking the Innocence from the Sunshine   11

of these sources. He knew when he heard God can save the biggest sinner that the preacher was talking about him. He knew if he did not accept Jesus, his life would end for eternity; and in hell, he would open up his eyes. As he sat in the pew with guilt written all over his face, he battled—the battle of life and death. As he sat in his seat, his heart started to burn, and that caused tears to roll down his eyes. His heart burned, and no water could put out the fire—not even the water that came from his own eyes. For the first time in life, he experienced hell.

He stood up and cried out for Tanya, and she went to hold him. But her love was not sufficient enough. The fire went from his heart to the depths of his soul. He cried harder, and the people from the church ran to his rescue. When he saw everybody coming to his rescue with water like firefighters, he thought that his fire would go out. But when every man and woman touched him, the fire grew worse and worse to the point of him fighting them off. He burned, and no water on earth could take out his fire. He cried and cried, "I need Jesus," as he ran up to the altar, turning around in circles and trying to put out the fire that now spread to all parts of his body.

He tried to fight all the demons, devils, and imps that lived within him. He fought and fought to put out the fire. But no matter how hard he fought, he could not put it out by himself. He stopped in the middle of the altar, dropped to his face, and rolled to Jesus's feet for his deliverance. Henry thought he was dead.

He cried, "I am a sinner, Lord, please forgive me for all my sins, and I will never do them again. I choose you from this point on in my life. I am prepared to deal with all the consequences of my actions. Please, just let me live."

He lay at Jesus's feet and cried for Him to help him. He looked at Jesus and said, "Please, bless me and let me live."

Jesus put out the fire with the water of the Holy Spirit. Jesus revived the Holy Spirit that lived within Henry that once was dead. Henry lay at the altar numb; he could not feel a thing. The angels could see the smoke rising from his body with all the demons that possessed him. The human eye only saw a sinful man, lying before God.

* * * *

Later that night while Sunshine was in her room watching TV, Henry stumbled up the stairs like a drunk man; but he was not drunk off of alcohol. He was high as a kite off the Holy Spirit that Jesus instilled in him at the altar.

Sunshine looked at him with fear in her eyes because she knew what was about to happen. He hugged her, falling from her arms, onto her legs and to her feet. He cried out, "I am sorry for killing you."

She did not understand what he meant at the time; but as she grew from a girl to a young lady to a woman, she

Taking the Innocence from the Sunshine   13

would fully understand and learn to hate him.

He got himself together because he realized she was puzzled by his words and actions. He said slower, "I am sorry for doing what I did to you. I will never do it again. Do you forgive me?"

Sunshine looked at him with un-forgiveness in her eyes and said, "Hell no."

Henry began to cry again, holding Sunshine's hand asking her, "Why?"

She started to cry out. "I hate you. I hate you. I hate you and my mother. I hate you because you did that to me, and my mother for not leaving you when I told her and moving you in with us. I hate you and my mother."

He held Sunshine's hand, hoping she could pull him to safety; but she just released the rope of life, causing his pride to die. He said, "Would you please forgive me? I promise I would never do that to you again. Please, Sunshine, forgive me.

She looked at him and said, "No, I will never forgive you—nor my mother."

He said, "Please don't be mad at your mother for my mistakes. Your mother loves you."

She replied with hurt, guilt, and shame in her eyes. "If she loves me, she would have left you."

He told her, "It is not that easy. The only thing that I can do is pray that God softens your heart and gives you to Jesus." He gave her two books—one was the Bible, and the other one was titled, *Introduction to Poetry*. As he walked through the streets in pain, he said, "Maybe you can find closure, healing, and deliverance in those books."

It doesn't matter who dies

Silence
Must not tell a soul.
This story must remain untold,
Never to unfold.
Burning skeletons
Never becoming whole,
For the enemy now has control.
And I must find my peace
Through this thing called poetry.
My pain I release

I write metaphors,
So he don't catch a felony,
And she can live out her dreams.
I die
By lethal injection
Because they had a connection.
Even though when she looked at me she sees
her own reflection.

She was not my way out,
Leaving me to restore my soul
Through this thing called poetry.
Hoping it will get me to see the heaven's gates,

Harvesting hate,
Because they are soul mates.
She'd rather walk blind
Because true love is hard to find.
True love always out lives death.
It doesn't matter who dies.
Right?

So I write rhymes
That rhyme on time,
And find hooks to save my own life.
Learning how to fight
Through the power of my tongue.
Spiting death so young
Because this story must remain untold,
Never to tell a soul.
Must not unfold
And face the truth.

I deal with the pain,
Like a growing wisdom tooth.
But through this thing called poetry,
I treat my pain with Novocain.
Writing on lined pieces of paper,
Ground I gain,
Speaking truths,
Breaking chains,
Scripting my pathway,
From going insane.
Through this thing called poetry,

Taking the Innocence from the Sunshine   17

Freedom I obtain
Because she was emotionally drained,
And saw no other trains coming
Her way.

They had a connection,
Even though when she looks at me she sees
Her own refection.
So she'd rather walk blind
Because true love is hard to find,
And true love always out lives death.
It doesn't matter who dies.
Right?

Beautiful flower

From the time of her birth, I apologized for my careless mistakes and asked God to forgive me for conceiving her in sin and having her out of wedlock.

After I watched the nurse's report me and my beautiful flower to the 2003 Census report, "Teenage mother on welfare, unmarried," I knew I would have to break the statistic that I placed upon myself—teenage mother with a high school education. Looking into her eyes, I knew I had to break the generational curse for my grandchildren. The love I have for her is overwhelming and unconditional. For the moment I laid eyes on her pink skin, big brown eyes, and red lips, I was blessed to know that God chose me to play the biggest part of her life: transforming from a girl trying to find her way to a woman with responsibility. I looked into her eyes and called her Ayanna, which is an African name and means beautiful flower. She was the beautiful flower in my dried up life. The love of my life that taught me how to love myself. She gave me purpose in life to the best of my ability. She gave me hope for a brighter tomorrow—just to know that a beautiful flower can grow in such a dry place. Her life convinced me that there was going to be rain in my life that would fertilize all the dry roots that had been buried

Taking the Innocence from the Sunshine 19

in me, caused by a painful past. Her cry was the vocal cords in my unheard voice. She brought out the unspoken words that I tried to say, but couldn't, because I felt I didn't have any support.

Before her, I felt like second was good enough; but for her, I will give my best to finish first. She will be my biggest cheerleader in life; her big brown eyes will push me to the finish line first. Now, I will live beyond my own expectations because of hers.

Taking the Innocence from the Sunshine 21

My First love on earth

It's so easy to say I love you,
My first love on earth.
You are a dream come true,
Changing my life at your birth.

My first love on earth,
My love for you is so strong,
Changing my life at your birth.
Giving you life can't be wrong.

My love for you is so strong
That the angels sing to your name.
Giving you life can't be wrong.

A true mother I have become.
The angels sing to your name.
You are a dream come true.
A true mother I have become.
It's so easy to say I love you.

Letting go

Loving you was so hard.
My heart wanted to hold on,
But my mind was saying let go,
Causing my mouth to say silly things,
Like begging you to stay with me.
Losing my dignity,
Becoming less than a woman,
Which I said I would be,
Acting foolish over a man.
Losing me
And my spirituality.
My eyes were closed.
Now I see.
You were keeping me from my destiny.

I put so much into you.
Not leaving none of me.
Drafting always from my poetry.
Cutting off all friends,
No family do I see
Because I thought you loved me.
Isolating my world,
So it can only be you and me.
Upsetting myself when I thought

Taking the Innocence from the Sunshine 23

You wanted to step outside my world,
My dream world,
My fantasy world,
That you-and-me-perfect world.

You and I
When we died
I cried.
For today
Because all the love went away .For all the good times
and bad,
For it is so hard to say goodbye to yesterday.

So, I cry for yesterday.
For all the times I should have cried,
For all the candy coating,
Me yearning
For something more
Outside our fantasy world.
I cry for tomorrow,
Wondering would this bring
My out-of-wedlock child sorrow.
Wondering if she would make the same mistakes as me.
But what can I say?
If I don't go the right way.

While I cry for today, yesterday, and tomorrow,
I breathe out relief
Because the Lord took a big load off of me,
Past what the eyes can see.

My love is forever lasting long

With the world behind me and her beside me,
The pressure is always on.
My mind stays going
On to the next move.
I can't lose,
For I have too much to lose
And I have already lost too much.
Like time,
And time is ticking.
No time for wasting
'Cause dreams are passing.
I have to catch them
For she is in front of me,
Beside me,
Wherever I move, she is there.
And she is not going anywhere.
For she is here.

She holds my future,
My destiny.
She gives me motivation
In her eyes
to move forward
And to never look back.

Taking the Innocence from the Sunshine 25

I am blessed
Because I have become what I have lacked.
For my life was in a shipwreck,
And self-love was gone.
My love for her taught me
How to love myself.
God gave her the keys
To bring the beauty out of me.

With the world behind me,
And her beside me,
In front of me,
The pressure is on.
But my love for her is forever lasting long.

Suicide

Generational Heartbreak

For he don't understand why,
And question himself every day,
Of how he can destroy this young girl's life.
And he never looked at another,
In this type of way.
And his questions remain unanswered,
Even though he is saved.
The past comes to haunt him
And steal his joy,
Like a thief in the night.

She wants to believe he was telling the truth,
And doesn't want to leave.
But wants the mother-to-daughter love.
But in life, you can't have your cake and eat it too.
Never did she want,
Her daughter to hate her
Like she hated her father.
Never did she want to have to face
The crossroad that her mother had to face.
But she was not strong enough to deal with the pain,
So she never crossed the crossroad
That was in her face.
She got sick,

The pain was too thick,
So she played it off like she was tricked.
The crazy things love makes you do
And refused to leave
Because he was all she knew.

Now I am the protector,
And I protect my herb
From the predator.
For I am the editor,
And she will not sing the same song.
But I sing the same song my mother sings,
For I have needs,
Performing wicked deeds,
Allowing wicked seeds
To come inside of me.
For her, I prefer one night stands,
So I keep a man-free zone,
Cover her eyes,
Like she thought she was covering mine.
But sight is given to the blind.
He had to leave by the crack of dawn,
And I'd rather meet the devil
At a hotel and leave her at home,
than have my daughter feel the hands
That me and mother once felt.

A true relationship we can't have
Because I don't believe he is telling the truth.
And he will never understand why

Taking the Innocence from the Sunshine

Because he don't look at little girls that way.
And I don't know no other way
To break this generational curse.
Because I don't want to face
My grandmother and mother's heartbreak.

LUCIFER WAS SO BEAUTIFUL TO HER. She never met a man who made her feel the way that he did. He talked with intelligence; but in reality, he was brilliant in lies, and she knew it. He fed her all his lies; and still, she ate them up like a moist, juicy steak.

She made mental love with him. Knowing her mind was being corrupted with dirty thoughts. That was not like God. She let sin penetrate her mind, causing her to fill herself with negative people and thoughts. She started to load bullets in the gun of death. He brainwashed her to think transgression was okay if she had reason behind it. Plus, her God would forgive her.

He would ask her if she loved him, knowing she would say yes. So, he told her to do all types of things to belittle herself, and she would—just so he wouldn't leave. For another heartbreak, she just could not bear. For she knew him so well and she knew he would always come back in her time of need. To give her a temporary Band-aid.

She became one with sin in the mind as Lucifer talked sweet nothings into her ears, filling her brain with pollution. She started to cover up his lies and made them seem right because she was blinded by the pain of

Taking the Innocence from the Sunshine   33

heartbreak. For she wanted to be somebody before her time of growth. He was the only one that lied to her and made her something she wasn't before her time. So, she lied to herself and became one with sin because it was so easy to do.

For there was not any direction put in place for her to follow. There were no parents to obey. No order, no one to turn to, and the footsteps placed before her—she hated. Causing her to convert herself to Lucifer, and she wasn't. For she was a god not yet manifested. Preparing to kill herself in sin with the loaded gun to her head. Becoming an adulterous wife because she could not see the unseen love of the God and the one He sent, Christ.

Putting Lucifer before God's Word of truth. He started to rub on her; rubbing some of his ways off on her. He rubbed his hand through her sweet hair and touched her in ways to blow off her head. He started to rub her body down with sin on the outside, but that was not enough— he had to get inside of her. He had to kill her. So, he started to kiss her sweet, innocent lips. Then the Lord came to her and said, "I love you."

At the time, Lucifer was so real. She pulled back from Lucifer. She said, "Lord, if you love me, deliver me."

He told her, "Deliver yourself, and stop sinning."

But sin felt so good to her flesh. Disobeying her Father in heaven, she started to make love with Lucifer. They started to undress each other and kiss each other up and down. She started to make love with sin as the gun rotated. He wanted her to feel something she had never felt before on earth, so he started to taste her insides and drinking all her innocent juices, so he could live. He needed the righteous to die and to stay alive, and another mission was about to be accomplished. Putting aside all the things God had done for her, she accepted sin like a pink piece of bubble gum. It was so sweet to her lips; it tasted so good to her tongue that she wanted another piece of Lucifer, another piece of the devil, and another piece of evil. She was about to OD on sin.

She could not pull sin from inside of her. She was too far gone into sin. It felt so good; it was so beautiful to her. She started to moan, "God damn, Lucifer. Give it to me, baby."

He lied to her, saying he loved her, and he would never leave her again.

She made sweet love with sin. As she was making love with Lucifer and he was imparting sin inside of her, she was pulling the trigger to the loaded gun. Killing her soul in sin, killing herself in sin, and reproducing the devil.

Taking the Innocence from the Sunshine   35

They are not him

How can I tap into his mind
If I can't tap into minds?
Reminded every time my pen don't hit the paper right.
My poetry just don't flow,
Retained my soul
To be transformed,
One step ahead.

But temptation
By the desire to have something unseeing,
Wanting him to make love to me
When I don't even know how
To make love to myself.
Self-love is gone because
I am trapped into him,
And I don't know
Who he is to be,
But a fantasy
Lost.

So I looked for him
On a one-way street,
Losing me,
The things that make Sunshine.

Settling
And populate myself with mean less faces
As they are leaving my contaminated bed without a trace.
And when I realize they are not him,
I drop them
Like calls lost on a cell phone.
But my soul can't erase them,
So I deteriorate .

Taking the Innocence from the Sunshine **37**

AS I WALKED UP TO THE FRONT DESK with my two forms of identification, I trained my heart to become numb. As I walked into the room of long-faced, conscious women and men, everyone in the room looked emotionally drained from the services of death they just paid for. We all sat in the room and looked at each other with guilt until our name was called.

Once my name was called, I went to the back, and the nurse asked me, "Are you sure you want to do this?"

I said, "Yes," but I really wanted to say no. But then I thought about being another single mother, another man, another, and my selfishness said, "Yes, I am sure." Then I gave her the rest of the money to kill my unborn child.

She said, "Okay, now you will go down to the second floor and take your medication."

I walked down to the second floor and got my pills from the nurse to begin the process of breaking my heart— and took a seat among different women for 45 minutes. All the women in this room were zoned out. Some were hooked up to IVs, some were asleep, and some were like me high off of drugs. Every woman in that room was high, zoned, gone from the reality that they were about to kill their own child. It was like a crack house. No more tears to be shed. No one had a conscience at that point; we all had to woman up and prepare to kill our own flesh and blood.

Then the doctor called me to the back. They had me lie on a table like the one you see in the OBGYN office and spread my legs like I was getting a pelvic exam. High as a kite, I just followed orders. The first minute they started the vacuum, and I felt a lot of pressure. And a minute later, I felt a very bad cramp; and the minute after that the doctor said, "Here is your dead baby." I looked in the square, silver pan of blood and saw my little seed. Within three minutes, I killed my child.

The nurse helped me put my clothes on and escorted me to the recovery room. I sat down in a recliner chair. It seemed like that three minutes took so much out of me. It took so much out of my soul, my womb, and my spirit. The drugs started to wear off, and I started to have withdrawal. I wanted more drugs and another Band-aid to cover my open womb.

The nurse said, "Okay, Sunshine, you are ready to leave. Come back in one week to follow up, and here is a prescription for pain." I took it all and walked out the door.

If I was in your shoes

If I was in your shoes,
There are so many things
I would do just not to lose.
But I will never know until the day comes
When I am in your shoes.
And how will I know if I will do better
If I am never put in your shoes?

It's like a blood line, generational relay race—
Pass the baton of burdens
From you to me
Because the load was too heavy.
How do know if I can carry the banner of truth,
Of pressure put upon you,
And win this race
At the finish line of justice
If I never pay my dues
And walk in your shoes?

Seeming you could not play
The hand you were dealt
For me and your granddaughter.
I hate to step in your shoes
For my grandchildren,

And I pray for God's graces to breathe upon me
So I don't have to step in your shoes.
But how do I know if I am better,
If I never walk up your ladder
Like you walked up mine,
And commit the same crime,
If I never walk in your shoes?

I question myself,
Is it better to sleep with the devil
Than to walk like you?
Is it better to live without a husband
Because of fear
Or walk down your road?
Would I rather have one night stands
Than to step my feet into your shoes?
Fucking partners as friends,
So I don't have to carry your cross.
Crucify my children like they did Christ.
Do I choose wrong over right?
Death over life?
Break all the rules?
Just not to walk in your shoes.
Do I despise you so much,
And hate the fact of being you?
I walk just like you
Down the same road,
Sharing the same story.
Do I lose
With the same pair of shoes?

Forgiveness

AS I WALK THROUGH THE VALLEY of the shadow of death, I walk in fear; and I fear all evil. As I walk through the valley, I walk scared, thinking about what is about to happen to me. As I take each step, I think about my life and what I have become in life. As I take each step, I ask myself, "Did I live a godly life?" As I take each step, I wonder if I am going to hell. As I take each baby step, I wonder: *Will I see Jesus?* Then I think about when I was saved at the age of seven; then I got saved at the age of eleven, and now I am twenty-four and dead because I could not play the hand life dealt.

As I walk through the wide valley alone with millions of other people, I walk at a slow pace scared of what my future holds. The valley is so busy like the New York City streets. The valley is bigger than the world itself. The valley has no smell, and it looks like nothing. People are standing on air, and there are no sidewalks, no trees, no grass—nothing but air. It is like closing your eyes and seeing nothing but pitch black. All material things are gone; the valley is so clear. It is nothing but air, my soul, and my flesh. I can actually look at my soul, and what it has become in life. It is black and has black smoke coming from it. I wonder why my soul would die in 2010; I cannot believe I killed myself at twenty-five. The valley has a lot of angels, directing traffic, pointing people in the line they are supposed to be in. The tallest angel points at me and says, "You need to be in the left line."

So I go in the left line. The left line is much longer than the right line. I walk through the valley of the shadow of death, fearing all evil but God. In life, I really did not fear God because I knew He would always forgive me. Finally, Jesus stands before me, and He stands there so beautiful. He is not white or black—He is all the colors and all the nationalities. I've never seen a man who looked like Him on earth. He has jet black hair and locks that flow down to His feet. He wears a purple robe with a gold string holding it together. He is six feet tall and about two hundred pounds. His mouth, nose, eyes, and ears fit perfectly on His perfect round face. His arms are cut just right. He has big hands and long fingers, and He has the cleanest fingernails. He has no shoes on His feet. His feet are even beautiful. He looks better than all the angels in heaven and all the humans on earth. At this point, even His name is beautiful. I just want to touch His face

As I go to hug Jesus, He moves away like I am a stranger. Like I did not exist in His world at all. I say, "Jesus talk to me. It's me, Sunshine, your child." Jesus just looks at me and does not say a word. He looks at me with tears in His eyes. He looks at me as if I was His only child, and He lost me. Tears start to pour from His eyes, causing it to rain on earth. His tears flood the United States of America, Germany, and for the first time in

Taking the Innocence from the Sunshine   45

years, Africa gets rain. His tears come down like He suffers a broken heart, and I am the one who broke His heart. He is trying to talk, but the words will not come out. It is like His words are stuck in the back of His throat. So, He closes His mouth, and we stand in silence.

I start to cry because I know that I just lost my only friend. My heart feels a pain it never felt on earth. It feels like a hundred knives are stabbing me in the heart. I feel my body deteriorate, and my soul burn. That is why there is so much black smoke coming from my soul because it is about to burn in hell. I cry, "Lord, please talk to me."

Jesus just looks at me like I am the devil. For the first time in my life, I fear the Lord because for the first time, He is real. The tears will not stop coming, and I cry out to Jesus and beg Him to talk to me.

Then He says, "You hold un- forgiveness in your heart, so you cannot enter the kingdom of heaven. Your un- forgiveness for man has driven you to kill yourself. You thought I was so far away, but I was right there. My Word says you need a mustard seed of faith to enter the kingdom of heaven. How do you have a mustard seed if you took matters in your own hands and killed yourself? Did you not trust me? Your breakthrough was on the way. No vacancy departs from me for I know you not." Then, He turns His back on me because He could not bear the pain.

Two demons come from behind a little, black door that has a tiny, brown doorknob. I did not see the door when I was walking through the valley. It must have appeared when Jesus said, "No vacancy." The two demons are deformed, and blood comes from their bodies. Half of their bodies are gone; it looks like a dog has been eating on their bodies. They come at me like they are happy to have me. They run at me like I am a football someone just fumbled. Before I can put my feet together to run away from them, I am in their arms. I yell and scream at the top of my lungs.

They drag me across the air like a rag doll. For the first time in life, air has a feeling. It feels like they are dragging me across concrete. For the first time in life, air looks like something. I see blood that comes from my body streak across the air. I fight like I never fought before and escape their arms. I run to Jesus; and as I am running, the demons grab me by my ankles, causing me to fall, and they drag me. I am so close to Jesus, so I squirm on the floor kicking my legs. I just want to touch Jesus's robe like the woman with the issue of blood did. So, I kick and kick until I am able to touch His robe. When I touch His robe, the demons let me go instantly, but my hands went right through Jesus's robe. The demons notice that my hands went right through His robe, and they grab me. I scream, "Please, Jesus, I am sorry; please forgive me."

The Holy Spirit says to me, "Jesus loves you so much that He is giving you one more chance to live life right."

Taking the Innocence from the Sunshine   47

As I travel down my mother's birth canal, I cry. "I want to be with Jesus."

Then the doctor says, "It's a girl."

And my life begins all over again.

Why should I die?

For when I hate you,
I hate myself.
Never can I fly
Mentally trapped in a hole,
Un-forgiveness lingers in my soul.
I refuse to give you that much control.
Killing me is your goal.
Why should I die?
Go to hell,
Enough tears I have cried.
Why should I die?

I don't understand why.
I participate in this hate race.
Emotions already crucified
And restricted by grace.
I refuse to give you victory
Because I can't look past history.
Why should I die?
Go to hell,
Enough tears I have cried.
Why should I die?

Hearing my blessing.

Taking the Innocence from the Sunshine 49

Because of my un-compassioned soul,
Past notes I review
And stay stuck in chapters.
So I never accomplish my happily ever after.
To others, I spray mace,
That boomerangs back into my face.
I fill myself with deadly poison.
My walk to the altar was pointless
'Cause I harvest hate.
My happiness I can't pursue,
My freedom is overdue
Why should I die?
Go to hell,
Enough tears I have cried
Why should I die?

Inside of me, so much shame
From past pain.
The Bible says the tongue no man can tame.
I have said words I can't replace,
Past actions I can't erase,
I take the full blame,
To God—I have prayed.
So who else do I owe allegiance to?
To myself I must stay true.
What else is there for a woman to do?
Why should I die?
Go to hell,
Enough tears I have cried
Why should I die?

For now and forever

Lord, you know me better than I know myself.
In the past, I thought I knew
What I wanted.
But I was too selfish to find out the errors lie within me.
I made up in my mind what I thought he should be.
But when I met him, I didn't like him.
And when I left him,
I didn't know myself.
I adapted to the ways of the world
That brought jezebel out of me.
So please build patience in me like Sarah.
They say you can't turn a hoe into a housewife,
But if you did it for Rahab, you can do it for me.
Rearrange the vines
That cause the blood to flow to my mind,
To become a Proverbs woman.

I ask you to build my righteousness man.
Let him love me
Like Christ loved the church.
Let him fear you like David.
Be as wise as Solomon.
Let him write me love, poetic scriptures.
Let his beauty appeal to me like Samson.

Taking the Innocence from the Sunshine   51

Open his mind's eye and ears.
Spear our tears over the years.
Let him be obedient like Noël;
So when you say move, he listens
And leads our family into riches
Like Abraham.
Let him lead our mind to the islands in Cleveland, Ohio.
Be his peace
In this time of pain,
Because he is missing the part
That lies within me.
Let him long for me,
Like Adam desired Eve.
The reason I know because he holds the 180 to me.
He and I make 360.
Making the half of us complete.
Let our love be concrete,
And let us fight the war of life

With the armor of GOD,
Against man and death,
Breathing in the same breath.
Enjoying each other's company
In love, even in eternity.
Redemption

I JUST PASSED THE FIRST CHECKPOINT in the spirituality race called faith. Running with my Bible, my sword, my rock and salvation in my hands. Talking, teaching, and preaching about my salvation. Wanting people to look at me run that good race called faith with my helmet of salvation, my belt of the truth that I could not buckle, and my shoes of the gospel that I could not tie. I felt like I was entitled to run, approved to talk because some people never saw Jesus, and I did. Not understanding I was just awarded a paid-in-full scholarship to the University of Christ. But, I still needed to act right and study to show myself approved. For I did not have time to learn how because I saw Jesus. Studying this faith took too long, and I just wanted to get in the race called faith to make up for lost time. In my arrogance, my pants fell to my ankles, and I tripped over my unlaced shoe strings.

Tears started to flow from my eyes, and my hands started to grab my Bible, my sword, my rock and salvation. My heart was saying God, please don't leave me. I am so sorry I can't run this race called faith alone. I tried and did nothing but fail you and myself. I tried all types of methods of redemption, but I still bleed. I cried like a child, "I just want a Band-aid."

Taking the Innocence from the Sunshine 53

I cried on the Bible until somebody came to hold me, and I stopped crying instantly. Even though I knew God, what He had done for me, and what He brought me through, I still felt like I could not go through life without a Band-aid being on my open womb. But that was where I failed because I needed major surgery—but afraid to go under the knife. Doping myself up with inertia and man made drugs. Not willing to bear labor pains and give natural birth to my redemption. That person stopped holding me once my weight broke his two limbs. I started to cry again because I did not want him to leave. I really did not want to hurt him. But hurt people hurt people. I was not ready to fight for my own deliverance. I'd rather cry like a child, "I just want a Band-aid for every cut and scrape of life." I cried: "Would somebody please come hold me?"

So, the devil sent demons that looked just like a man. I thought he was the man I needed. 'Cause nobody else came in my time of need. So he held me, and I held him. While he was holding me, I thought about all the people that were suppose to hold me. All the time they were suppose to be there, but they let me go in my time of need.

Still not learning from my mistakes. I held him tighter than the last person, place, or thing. Hoping he would not leave me like my mother and father left me. I put so much trust in him, and I did not even know what made up his name. I did not know if he was Devil, Lucifer, or Satan. For Jesus knew every hair on my head and loved me more then I loved myself. But I still could not trust Him in spite of all the things He had done for me.

Then I realized we were two hurt people trying to heal each other. Sooner rather than later, we let each other go. The pain between the two of us was unbearable for any human to bear, leading to the death of an unwanted child— that was made out of hurt and pain of past history.

The list of sin grew longer, and my faults expanded. Being looked at like a hypocrite became intense because I would always run back to my Bible, my sword, my rock and salvation. For I do understand, he could not hold me and hold himself up as well. I still cried of a broken heart because I put so much trust in him and such a little time just to be let go. A million preached sermons could not heal this open womb that bleed. I cried like a child, "I just want a Band-aid, somebody." I wanted anybody because I lacked self love. As I held the Bible, my sword, my rock and salvation tighter, harder and harder, and cried a sincere cry from the bottom of my heart, "Lord, please don't leave me. Please don't be temporarily in my life."

Like the man I slept with that left me at the crack of dawn. Or the man that so called loved me, so I had his baby and he left me to be a single mother. Or the man that wanted to marry me that left me for another woman and a deceased child. Like the alcohol that left me with a hangover the next morning.

Taking the Innocence from the Sunshine   55

Or the drugs that left me belittling myself as a woman for my next fix. I cried like a child, "I just want a Band-aid."

But I don't want to go back to where I came from. For I have come too far and accomplished too much not to trust you, Lord. I have not been transformed just to backslide down the road of discretion. I cried out, "I understand I need you Jesus and nobody or nothing else." I cried like a child, "I just want a Band aid."

For this race is hard, and my feet are weak. As I lay on the Bible, my sword, my rock and salvation.

Bipolar

Keep in bondage for so many years,
Releasing myself from jail.
It so easy to blame life on her, him, and them.
I'm retaining my freedom,
I'm standing strong and quitting being a victim.

When they are to blame
And everybody wants me to shut-up
And get off that shit.
But I'm emotionally sick.
I hear voices,
Craving
To be touched,
To be rubbed,
and bust a fat nut.

But God don't like that.
I hear voices—
Voices in my head.
I want to feel him,
But don't even know his name.
I'm a junkie who needs a fix.
I tried, but I can't quit.
It feels so good,

Taking the Innocence from the Sunshine 57

And I been feeling it for so long.
20 years—and I'm only 25.
I don't have an answer to why
'Cause I hear voices in my head.
I'm a junkie, looking for some good dick
For the devil is a liar—I will not be tricked,
God's grace is new every day.
And I want a relationship—
A husband.
But I don't,
'Cause
He don't understand.
And never look at little girls that way.
But I don't want to face my mother's heartbreak.
I just need a one night stand.
No, no, I'm celibate
'Cause niggas aren't shit.
I hear voices,
I need a quick fix.
Maybe,
Just maybe—porn and a toy
Will do the trick.
Being looked at like a hypocrite ,
'Cause I know God and His love set me free.
For the preacher said I have the victory,
And for that hour it made sense.
I am not the victim.

But I am the victim.
And no one understands.

But then a guy I met last week—
For we are soul mates,
And we going to run this life race.
The sex is great.
I'm his bitch.
But my name is Ms. Brown,
And I am an independent black queen.
I'm paying him like a crack head fiend.
Who in the hell does he think he is?
Baby, please don't leave.
But the Bible says I need a ring,
And the preacher said I can't love two gods.
So, fuck you.
But I been feeling good for so long,
And I need him to touch me at least once a week.
So, he thinks I'm crazy.

Why do they tell me to get over it?
Everybody wants to keep this under cover,
Leave it in the bed,
As I change lovers,
And hear voices in my head.
They draw the conclusion—
Bipolar is the disorder.
But that's an illusion,
And my medications are the solution
To my
Unanswered problem.

I am tired

I am tired.
Singing the same song,
Praying the same prayer,
Playing this game
Called church.
Myself is the only one I hurt.
It like going to school for eleven years and then
Dropping out
Because of doubt
And the lack of the mustard seed of faith.
It's like going to work every day with no pay.

The Word that is imparted into me week after week
After week, I shout
After months into years.
Wasted,
Living in vain,
Soul still destroyed.
Life I cannot enjoy
Because of disobedience.
I just can't get the correct ingredients
To the recipe of life.

I am the lost sheep,

Entrapped in slavery
Because I hear voices.
People whispering in my ear,
The Holy Spirit dwelling on conscience.
Lust cutting my hair,
Pain voiding my soul,
Hate harvesting my heart,
Causing me to run
To my addiction
And just deal with the conventions
Of being called a hypocrite.
For drugs that are man-made
And a Band-aid.

It's just unfair
If my life ends here.
For my iniquity
Will not have victory.
My heart is sincere
To do God's will
Even in my backsliding condition.
I beg for forgiveness
Like a man who is about to lose
His Proverbs wife.
I will pick up my heavy cross
And carry it down the road of life.
I ask for mercy time after time.
I plead the blood of Jesus Christ,
In these dark areas of my butterfly.
I speak color,I speak light,

Taking the Innocence from the Sunshine

I speak life,
So I can fully fly
In God's Word.
My history
Is no longer a mystery.
I laid it all down at the altar
I need more than a transformation.
Because of salvation,
The Bible says I will become a new creation.

Taking the Innocence from the Sunshine 63

Restless is my soul

Restless is my soul
Over my life I lose control
for I have been spiritually feed
Christ red blood has been shed
But I can't maintain my head
To look ahead
That's why my soul remain
Restless

For I have weather this this storm before
So I don't understand why I look back
Jump off track
My walk I trying to retain
In sin my the peace of God I can't maintain
Going backwards is insane
But addicted to pain like cocaine
That's why my soul remains
Restless

I kill myself with better knifes
And diminish my soul with every wind of life
Confusion my religion with worldly temptation
Questioning my salvation
Leading to my own frustration
That's why my soul remains
Restless

For I am saved
So he dwell in me
But when I depart from thee
Like Saul my rob is stripped to the bone
Restless is my soul
But it is destiny that I finish this race
So I play my harp threw poetry
Because of grace
He order my steps into perfection
But I weather give up sacrifice
Then to follow direction
That's why my soul remains
Restless

Taking the Innocence from the Sunshine   65

Don't cry for me

Don't cry for me
'Cause I'm not dead,
And don't bury me alive
'Cause of my story.
For this is what holds my loyalty.
So don't cry,
And don't feel my pain.
Don't wish for things to change,
And it was my destiny.
Just grow from my story.
For God gets all the glory.

Don't crucify me,
'Cause I already went to the cross.
I refuse for this story to be lost.
So I tell it,
And you feel my pain.
But don't cry for me.
I'm resurrected
Through Christ Jesus,
And your tears should dry for that reason.
So don't cry for me

Like you're standing over my casket at my funeral.
I rose from the dead.
for it I write hooks.
I write books,
and even if the innocents was killed
in the sunshine
the sun always raise again.
After every storm
The world knows that,
 the sunshine will raise again!

Checkout another book by Lytoni S. Brown

My name is Eve

My name is Eve
Came from my husband
Cause I am the mother
Of all living things
I am the coca cola shape body
Little tits
Nice hips
Conniving bitch

My name is eve
Came after I ate
from the good and evil tree
I was deceived by satin he thought me some good love
making
He showed me that I hold power over a man
That lies in between my legs
That is why I act all boogie
With my nose in the air
Because I hold the weapon in between my legs

As I was using my weapon
I was deterring my soul
As I was putting my children to rest
For I am the cause of there death
I suppose to be the mother of birth
But my children are dying
They went from living for internally
To nine hundred
To ninety-nine

Now they are dying at twenty five
And my weapon is the reason why
My children are dying
They are losing there mind
Some are walking around dead alive

Adam got tried of trying
Nothing is the truth
Now we both are lying
Deceiving the creator plan
Seeming Adam can't trust a women
He turn to man
But he can't stay always
So he comes back and infest my body with
AIDS
And my weapon is the reason why
Adam looks for love in every way
Form
And shape
Our daughter he rapes
She looks to release the pain
So she sex every man she dated
Following her mother sinful mistakes

 My son don't have much to look up to
Because his father is less then man
And he don't want to follow the trend
So he is intervene by the fast money making
He let go of his pain in dope
His life is burning like fire on a rope
When he is thirty- five
He will have nothing to show
Because of my sins my sons
Are dying young and broke

Transformation

Satin keep lying
I am conniving
Deceiving
To get what I want and need
Adam was not create for me
Knowing I hold power in between my legs
Ignoring the tears my children shed
Forgetting about the knowledge in my mind
Because it is easier to open my legs
Refusing to feed my brain
So I keep on having children I can't raise
Aborting them everyday
 In the clinic
And in other ways
Neglect my children needs
How selfish of me

My sins is a chain reaction
At the end I get no satisfaction
Satin laughing and relaxing
But I won't let his lies over power me
Because of Calvary
I have the power to change
And make tomorrow a band new day
For my name is Eve
And I am the mother of all living things

Turning her out

Innocent
Pure as snow
For she doesn't know
He shows her so many things
Sexually
He's twenty- two
She's sixteen
She thinks it's cool
To date an older man
He takes her from a child to a woman
She tell lies
And think of reasons why
And how to get to him
And feel that feeling
She never felt
The hugging
The kissing
The touching
The rubbing
The licking
He's working
His way to sticking
This young innocent child
Turning her out
Teaching her how to run wild

He says be quite it's not going to hurt
She doesn't know from this point

Transformation

Her life will be corrupt
From his after math
He makes her leave fast
So he can freshen up
For his next piece of young ass
She leave with dreams known they would last
She go home and calls him
But he don't return her calls
Because in his world she don't exists at all

Six weeks later
She lays on the doctor table
She tells him
She's contacted an STD
He says what dose that
Have to do with me
She says I thought you
LOVE me
He says baby
Lets be realistic
You think I love you
You are just another
statistic

Cold world alone

My family and friends are always
Even if I try it seem like they won't stay
My boyfriend has flown
I'm in a cold world alone

Where can I turn
Where no one shows concern
Their actions have shown
I'm in a cold world alone

The cold wind hit my face
It seem like my eyes are filled with mace
I feel like I 've been hit with a stone
I'm in a cold world alone

I walk in darkness hoping to see light
Wondering if things will ever get right
I can not return home
In this world I feel so alone

I cough because I have a chill
No one cares how I feel
Every body has grown
I'm this world I feel alone

Mt heart is broken
Actions and words has been spoken
My music has no tone

Transformation

I'm in a cold world alone

My head is puzzle
Over my body my loved ones put a muzzle
I feel as I 've been stripped to the bone
I'm in a cold world alone

LaVergne, TN USA
25 July 2010
190799LV00002B/1/P